GROWTH STRATEGIST'S GUIDEBOOK

Plan Before You Post, Publish or Pay-Per-Click

TIM KINNEY

DEDICATION

For my clients -- a continual source of inspiration and friendship.

CONTENTS

ACKNOWLEDGMENTS

For such a short and simple book, so many people have influenced its creation. I never formally studied business or marketing. I learned the trade on the fly from those much smarter and better skilled. I also do not consider myself a writer and writing a book didn't change that opinion. However, there are mentors, teachers, friends and family who generously share their wisdom with me, personally and directly. I thank you all. Specifically, I'd like to thank those from the early years in Solvay, New York: Karen Notcher, Carol Pouliot, Ed Sturdevant and Tom Leonardo. I'd also like to thank Gary Overvold, Don Riedel, J.P. Clark, Phil Meyer, Bruce Farmer, Phil Barackman, Dale Lois, Noel Ramos, Mike Fleet, Doreen Deary, Curtis Draper, Terry Rose, Mike Hanrahan, and Keith Zar.

Of course, nothing is possible without the love and support of my family. Thank you Andrea, Jake, Annette and Fran Birdsall, and my mother, Irene Bury.

And there are those mentors who have taught me through their writings whom I credit in the recommended reading section for each chapter.

Any and all failings (on marketing, strategic planning or writing) are my own. My apologies. I'll do better next time.

INTRODUCTION
(HOW I BECAME A MARKETING FUNDAMENTALIST)

"Do you think I should start a blog?"

"We ran some Google AdWords and it didn't work for us."

"We've got someone here on social media, but our sales are still flat I know social media is here to stay, but, in our business, it really doesn't impact growth."

"I don't even know where to start."

THESE ARE excerpts from recent conversations I've had with clients and prospects. Comments like these prompted me to write this book. They point to a need in the market for a back-to-basics approach to growth planning. There are thousands of tools to promote a business. But, does all that promotion lead to sustainable growth? What are your best options? What are the fundamental elements of a sound growth plan and what are the steps to create such a plan? Here's my quick assessment and some assumptions:

First, I take it for granted that most business owners want to grow their business (and for good reasons, which I won't get into here in depth.) Second, growing your business is not easy and even the best-educated, experienced business owner or executive may not have actually written a growth plan in a long time. They are looking for a place to start. Third, there are so many growth and marketing options available to businesses, so much technology, it has hard to see the forest for the trees. I am referring to the incredible opportunities we now have to promote our businesses from our desktops. Within minutes and for a few hundred dollars, we can launch a global advertising campaign from our desktops. It is so easy, we sometimes lose sight of what we were trying to accomplish in the first place. And, all too often it can spin out of control in a vicious circle – running ads to promote content that is intended to generate leads which then need more content to keep them engaged and nurtured, and so on.

But, in the midst of all this activity, we can never forget why we are doing it. We are here to help our customers solve a problem. And, to paraphrase Zig Ziglar, if we help enough people get what they want, we'll help ourselves get what we want.

And, that brings me back to why I wrote the guidebook. Quite simply, I wrote the guidebook to help my clients and friends grow their businesses. If I am being completely honest, writing the guidebook also helped me. It forced me to document my approach and it makes it easier to explain what I do, how I do it.

WHO SHOULD USE THE GUIDEBOOK

The Guidebook is ideal for business owners and leaders who want to grow a business and looking for the best place to start the growth planning process. It is for sales and marketing department leaders, entrepreneurs and business owners. In my experience, you want three things:

1.   a growth strategy
2.   a process to identify, evaluate and develop your strategic growth options
3.   a practical plan to execute the strategy

If that describes you, then you are what I call a Growth Strategist. This book is for you.

HOW TO USE THE GUIDEBOOK

This Guidebook is not intended to be a scholarly treatise on growth strategy or strategic planning theory. Instead, it is a simple and practical guide to the 10 most important elements of a successful growth plan for your organization. The Guidebook consists of 10 planning modules, organized into 10 chapters. Each chapter contains exercises designed to help you create those plan elements in 10 steps.

Completing each exercise will produce the information you need to formulate your strategy, and also generate a short, written plan. I strongly recommend that you complete all of the exercises in a Chapter per week. This will keep the planning process moving. And, without compromising quality, the faster you compete the plan, the sooner you can start growing.

Most of the exercises are based on probing questions about your business. That is, I ask you a lot (and I mean a lot) of questions. As you answer these questions, you are formulating your strategy and documenting it in a plan as you go. There are 11 types of workshop exercises in the Guidebook, including:

1. Brainstorm
Rapidly generate lots of ideas aiming for quantity, not quality. Typically, brainstorming is done as a group, but can also be done solo.

2. Hole Punch
Building on the principle that what doesn't kill the idea will make it stronger; Hole Punch harnesses the power of negative thinking to help look for problems and hidden complexities in your ideas.

3. Research
Many of the questions I'll ask don't always have obvious answers. You'll need to actively search for them. Some research can be done yourself. But, you may need to recruit expert help to conduct market studies, surveys, focus groups or find credible third-party published data reports.

4. Analysis
Sometimes the information you find in your research requires you to dig deeper into the material to find patterns and hidden truths.

5. Buddy Up
Don't go at this alone. Find a friend or trusted advisor with whom you can share your ideas, progress, concerns and fears. Your buddy can be anyone you trust, however, I recommend talking to an impartial source outside your organization.

6. Role-play
Do you hear what you sound like? Sometimes, an idea seems brilliant until you see another's reaction to what you've said. Try things out for size in a safe setting before you share it on the big stage. I also encourage you to record yourself (audio and video) and then watch the playback to find where your strategy and plan needs work.

7. Draft
It is crucial to commit your thoughts and ideas to paper. In fact, the art of

drafting your ideas will help clarify your thinking. If you can't communicate it intelligibly to someone else in written form, you probably don't fully understand it yourself. Take the effort to jot it down. Then, go back and rewrite until it is crystal clear. Your plan may go through several drafts before you are ready to launch.

8. Question
One of the most powerful planning tools in your planning tool kit is your ability to ask questions to make your strategy and plan stronger. Key power questions include:

a.   What's in it for me?
b.   So what?
c.   Why?
d.   How?
e.   What if..?
f.   What are you going to do about it?

9. Focus
Many exercises require you to dig deeper and concentrate on a particular exercise to better clarify, refine and crystallize your strategy.

I highly recommend that you complete the exercises in the order they appear in the Guidebook. The work and thought product from the early exercises is needed in the later exercises. For instance, skipping ahead to the Budget exercise in Chapter 9 will not do you much good since you don't have the tactical plan developed on which the budget should be based.

The exercises are based on the best practices, ideas, and processes that have worked well for me, and my clients over the past 26 years. Most of it is original and builds on my own experience – success and failure alike. However, I shamelessly borrow from friends, mentors and other consultants, sharing what has worked for them and their clients. I give credit where it is due. If I fail to cite a reference, accept my apologies. It is unintentional and a symptom of sloppiness and faulty memory. All mistakes in thought or judgment are my own.

Each chapter also includes a resource section in which I share my recommendations for further reading and online sources of helpful information. Finally, the most strategically healthy organizations are those that make the planning process part of their culture. My hope is that the method and tools provided in the Guidebook will help you build an active database of strategic options and as a template for developing future plans.

WARNING!

I've tried to make the Guidebook easy to use and easy to read. However, the work that will go into the exercises is not easy. I ask a lot of tough questions and I mean a lot of questions.

All in, there are 37 exercises in the Guidebook. Some of them will go quickly. Others may take you several hours over several days to complete in full. Many times, you may not know the answer and it may not be easy to find the answer.

But, I will make you a promise: the effort you put into the exercises will pay off in the end. The time and energy spent here will help you realize the growth you want.

Happy planning!

⌘

A GROWTH PLANNING CHECKLIST

You don't need a traditional 30-40-page plan to be successful. However, your growth plan should cover several critical elements. Here's a quick checklist to help track your progress as you go. Does your current growth plan cover all of these areas?

- ✓ SMART objectives
- ✓ Performance audit
- ✓ Gap analysis
- ✓ Customer analysis (demographics, needs, analysis, life patterns, decision map)
- ✓ Market & competitive analysis
- ✓ SWOT analysis
- ✓ Market openings
- ✓ Strategic options & evaluation
- ✓ Business value platform
- ✓ Unique selling proposition
- ✓ Competitive advantage
- ✓ Proof points
- ✓ Buyer's journey funnel
- ✓ Tactical action plans
- ✓ Forecast
- ✓ Budget

1 SMARTER S.M.A.R.T OBJECTIVES

When it is obvious that the goals cannot be reached, don't adjust the goals, adjust the action steps. —Confucius

WHERE TO start? Growth strategy starts with the end in mind. That is, what is it you want to accomplish? As the introduction to the Guidebook noted, all 10 modules are critically important. Without being too dramatic, the first module is of the utmost importance since the work you do here will shape where your organization is going and what you and your organization will do. In Chapter 1, you will define your strategic objectives.

Organizations without clearly defined, specific, and measurable objectives rarely succeed. At the risk of cliché, your strategic objectives are your North Star. They will guide you and your followers to your destination. It is up to you to make sure you chart a clear course and calibrate the compass.

CHAPTER 1 OBJECTIVES
By the end of session one, you will have a clear direction for your growth plan. You will:
1. Decide which plan type to create
2. Define several strategic & SMART objectives
3. Formulate your SMART objectives into challenge questions

Like the genie in a bottle, the answers to these challenge questions will shape your growth strategy. So, be careful what you ask for!

EXERCISE 1.1 FOCUS

CHOOSE THE RIGHT PLAN TYPE

The 30-40 page standard marketing or business plan format that we all know (and many hate) may not be necessary for you. For many companies, a skinny version of the plan with a companion presentation and supporting financial spreadsheets is all you need. In this first exercise, you'll determine which plan type is right for you. Based on the needs and requirements of whoever is going to read and use the plan.

EXERCISE 1.1

1. Use the flow chart below to determine the most appropriate plan type for you. For many businesses, a short executive summary, detailed spreadsheets and a simple presentation is all you will need to capture your growth strategy.

2. Don't go it alone. Based on the plan you selected, start recruiting some help. The more complex your plan, the more help you'll need. Take a look at the sample plan outline in the Chapter 1 Resources section and think about where you need more help. Go ahead and ask for help in advance and line up your support team now. Don't forget about the practical things like copywriting, formatting, designing the plan and developing a companion presentation. All of these tasks can take a lot of time.

EXERCISE 1.2 ANALYSIS
REVIEW YOUR PAST OBJECTIVES
In this exercise, you will review your past business objectives to determine if they are still relevant and valid. If they are, use these objectives as a starting point. We'll update them in exercise 1.3. But, if you did not have objectives or they are no longer valid, start from scratch!

EXERCISE 1.2 INSTRUCTIONS
1. Did you set objectives? If so, what were your organizations' past objectives? List them.

2. How did you know about these objectives? Think about how they were communicated to you. How will you communicate them better moving forward?

3. Did your organization achieve these objectives? Were the results communicated? Providing feedback on critical objectives is a strong motivator. How will you communicate progress and results in the future?

4. If you did not achieve the objectives, explore the reasons why.

5. Which objectives will you continue to pursue?

EXERCISE 1.3 BRAINSTORM
DEFINE YOUR OBJECTIVES
In this exercise, brainstorm additional objectives not captured in exercise 1.2. Think about your entire organization from top line revenue generation to bottom line profits. Don't forget to include all of the departments that will be impacted. Don't worry about being precise. We'll clean them up later.

EXERCISE 1.3 INSTRUCTIONS
1. Review your organization's Mission and Vision statements. What objectives need to be accomplished in order to make your vision a reality and achieve your mission?

2. What would you like to celebrate at the end of the planning period? How will you celebrate it?

3. What are your top line revenue goals for the planning period?

4. What are your net operating profit goals for the planning period?

5. Think about your financial objectives above, how will the other departments in your organization contribute to achieving these objectives? Consider HR, marketing, sales, operations, finance, customer service, etc. Draft at least one objective for each department.

EXERCISE 1.4 FOCUS
GET S.M.A.R.T.

Using the draft objectives you developed from exercises 1.2 and 1.3 now you will make them even better by applying the S.M.A.R.T. principle to each of them. That means your objectives should be specific, measurable, attainable, realistic, and timely.

EXERCISE 1.4 INSTRUCTIONS

1. Starting with your top line revenue objective, how can you make your objective more specific? Think about the objective in terms of the number of customers you need to generate or retain. You may also consider specifying which product or service lines the income should come from? Or, is there a particular geographic territory that you will focus on?

2. Specifically, when will you need to accomplish your objective? Set an exact date including month, date and year.

3. Now, ask yourself: are these newly framed objectives realistic and attainable? If not, why not? How would you change them?

4. Would extend the time period? Lower them?

5. How will you measure your progress and results? Do you have the internal capacity and tools to monitor and report on your progress? What changes are needed in order to better track your success?

6. Repeat steps 1-5 for all of your objectives.

EXAMPLE:

Suppose you want to increase your top line revenue to $10,000,000. So, your first draft of your strategic objective might be:

Generate $10 million in annual revenue.

Where will this revenue come from – a specific region or territory? Existing customers or new customers? Are you making ten $1 million dollar deals or 1 million $10 sales? Is there a target profit level? What is the deadline? As you think through these questions to make it a SMART objective, it becomes:

Generate $10 million is annualized contract value through 20 new customers in the Southeast with 15% EBITDA by December 31, 2016.

EXERCISE 1.5 HOLE PUNCH, ROLE PLAY & BUDDY UP

Take your newly minted smart objectives and unleash the power of negativity by punching holes in them. Don't hold back. What doesn't kill them will make them stronger. Then, once you've had a go, share them with a trusted friend or advisor and ask for their opinion. Did he or she see something you missed?

EXERCISE 1.5

1. Pretend you are an attorney. Are there any legal issues with your objectives?

2. Pretend you are your biggest competitor. Do you see any weaknesses with your objectives?

3. Pretend you are your biggest supplier. What problems do you see with your objectives?

4. Pretend you are your biggest customer. How will these objectives impact them? Will service suffer if you get bigger?

5. Update your objectives once you've punched some holes in them to make them stronger. Then, share them with a trusted advisor. What is his/her reaction? Did (s) he offer any helpful suggestions? How will you change your objectives based on the feedback?

EXERCISE 1.6 QUESTION
REFRAME YOUR OBJECTIVES AS QUESTIONS

Now that you have a clearer idea about what you want to accomplish, you probably have a really big question on your mind: How are we going to do it? This question is deceptively simple but incredibly powerful. In fact, this line of questioning will drive the development of your strategy and tactical plans.

EXERCISE 1.6

1. Rewrite all of your SMART objectives as "How...?" questions.

Example:

Using the updated example I shared in Exercise 1.4, here's how it reads as a challenge question:

How will we generate $10 million is annualized contract value through 20 new customers in the Southeast with 15% EBITDA by December 31, 2016?

EXERCISE 1.7 DRAFT

You are almost done with Chapter 1. Great job! Now, compile all of the work from exercises 1.1 through 1.6 and write it up.

EXERCISE 1.7

1. Create a new document or a spreadsheet and draft up your SMART objectives.

2. Then add your challenge questions to the document.

3. Make sure to protect your objectives by storing them in a password protected file or location.

4. Save your work and make sure you have a password protected backup file.

You may not realize it now, but by completing these first seven exercises, you have done something profoundly good for your organization. Your SMART objectives and challenge questions have given your employees focus. Even at this early stage, they now know where they are going and what they need to do. Their jobs make more sense and take on new meaning. And, they know what their priorities are. First, they need to answer the challenge question!

⌘

CHAPTER 1. RESOURCES

SAMPLE PLAN OUTLINE

- Executive Summary
    - Goals & Objectives
    - Current Situation & Gap Analysis
    - Challenges, Roadblocks, obstacles in the path to success that must be overcome
- Target Audience Analysis
    - Research Summary (primary & secondary research highlights)
    - Demographics
    - Target Personas
    - Key Drivers/Motivators
- Industry & Competitive Analysis
    - Market size, Trends, Cycles, Value chain summary
    - Key industry players (by type and specific operators)
    - Competitive analysis
    - SWOT Analysis
- Strategy
    - Vision, Market opening / Big Idea / Strategy
    - Value Platform, Competitive Advantages, Proof points (for every competitive advantage), Key Messages By Audience
    - Buyer's Decision Journey & Conversion Funnel(s) by Target Type
    - Key Performance Indicators (KPI's by Conversion Funnel Stages)
- Integrated Tactical Marketing Plan (By Buyer's Journey Conversion Funnel)
    - Timetable (Weekly/Monthly, By Conversion Funnel Stages)
    - KPI Metrics Dashboard
- Budget & Financials

PLAN SELECTOR FLOWCHART

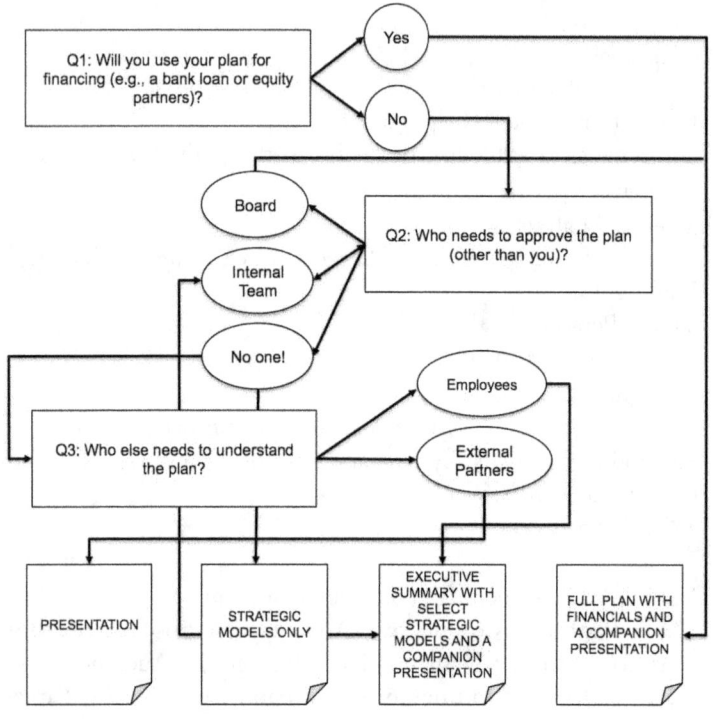

RECOMMENDED READING

A More Beautiful Question, Berger, Warren, 2014.

Leading With Questions, Marquardt, Michael, 2014

The One Page Business Plan, Horan, James. 2004.

S.M.A.R.T Goals Made Simple, Scott, S.J. 2014

SMART Goals: The Ultimate Goal Setting Guide, Gudger, Jacob. 2013.

2 GAP ANALYSIS & PERFORMANCE AUDIT

Half the money I spend on advertising is wasted. The trouble is, I don't know which half. -John Wanamaker

NOW THAT you know where you are going, guided by your challenge question and SMART objectives, analyzing where you've been sheds tremendous insight. If applied, those insights can save you from repeating costly mistakes. You will also make sure that you take what's working to the next level. Going from your current state to your target state may feel overwhelming, like crossing a chasm. So, don't make a leap of faith like Indiana Jones. Take a more analytical approach and measure the distance carefully, map out the best steps to take and consider what challenges lie ahead.

CHAPTER 2 OBJECTIVES
By the end of Chapter 2, you will:
- Audit your past growth performance and establish baseline metrics
- Know your current growth costs
- Refine SMART Objectives
- Identify and solve challenges, obstacles, and potholes before you execute your strategy

EXERCISE 2.1 ANALYSIS
PAST PERFORMANCE AUDIT

Now is the time to take stock of what's working and what's not in order to optimize your growth engine. But first, you've got to have the data. In this exercise, you'll take a peek under the hood at the two critical components of your growth power source, sales and marketing. This is labor intensive if you aren't already keeping track. So, you may need some help from your team.

EXERCISE 2.1

Select a specific time period for your performance review. You will likely need to go back 12-36 months to get enough information in order to identify meaningful patterns. Longer review periods will give you a better chance at spotting trends but it will take more effort. Depending on how deep you want to dwell, you may need some help. This is a perfect assignment for a team member that likes research, data and analysis. Here's what to look for:

1. Sales Performance Data

This will vary based on your business model and sales process, but, generally you are looking for your sales organization's performance statistics related to closing sales (volume/customers and revenue), proposals issued, presentations delivered, inbound and outbound sales calls, etc.). Essentially, you will need data for all sales activity required to make a sale. And, you'll need to make sure that the data includes the same level of specificity as your SMART objectives (including product/service type, geography, customer type, etc.).

2. Marketing Performance Data

Next, pull all of your marketing data for the corresponding time period. (Depending on the length of your sales cycle from lead generation to close, you may have to extend the length of the assessment period to capture corresponding marketing information to closed sales.) You will need to capture your lead generation activity -- everything from advertisements, promotions, e-mail campaigns, events, public relations, social media, etc. and their related performance statistics. See the Chapter 2 Resources section for a sample list of data points.

NOTE: If you don't have this information, the bad news is your business essentially fails this portion of the audit. And, it is going to be impossible to make data driven-decisions. The good news is you have less work to do in this chapter and you can add a new objective to your list: implement a better growth data metrics system!

3. Now that you have the data, conduct a quick assessment of each of the measured factors. Using a simple sliding scale (e.g. from 1 to 5 where 5 is the best), rate the effectiveness of your sales and marketing performance. For instance, one simple way to evaluate performance activity is to ask, "How well is _____ working to achieve my growth objectives?" Repeat this question for each activity or initiative.

If you've captured the data in a database workbook (recommended) like Excel, Google Sheets or a more sophisticated database program, you can add a rating column to capture your assessments activity by activity.

4. Next, for each of your assessments, investigate why the effort is or is not working well. For now, don't worry trying to solve the challenges. At this point, it is good enough to identify some preliminary issues and challenges.

5. Based on your initial review, what are the top three performing elements in both your sales and marketing engines? Brainstorm at least one way you can make each of the top 3 even better.

6. Now identify which are the worst performing elements in your sales and marketing engines. Are they essential? Can these components be fixed? If not, can they be stopped? What are the implications if you stop them?

7. If you have recently conducted any customer performance surveys or scorecards, this information should be included here as well.

8. Using these assessments, update, add to, delete from or reprioritize your SMART objectives list.

EXERCISE 2.2 ANALYSIS

CALCULATING COSTS & ROI

We are striving for as close to exact costs per new lead to customer acquisition in your current growth program. To get a more accurate read, this should include in-house and outsourced labor costs in addition to sales and marketing related expenditures. This will become very important later when we are evaluating other growth options.

EXERCISE 2.2

1. Using the spreadsheet you developed in Exercise 2.1, add another column and enter the related costs for each of the growth activities you are investing in. Of course, exact data is desired but ballpark estimates are acceptable at this point (as long as you go back and clean it up later).

2. With this information, you can now determine (roughly) your estimated costs per new customer, cost per lead, and the cost of conversion from lead to sale. Crunch these numbers several ways. First, calculate costs including your sales and marketing staff overhead. Then, calculate the costs after omitting your internal sales team or marketing team. This will help illustrate the impact of each on your overall growth ROI. If you improved your conversion rates, what is the impact on your results? You now have a clearer idea of the current investment you are making to grow your business and what results you get from that investment.

3. Now, using this information, can you identify potential opportunities to reduce costs, improve conversions, or accelerate the new business cycle? Update your SMART objectives, incorporating your new insights from your cost review.

EXERCISE 2.3 ANALYSIS
GAP ANALYSIS, BUDDY UP & BRAINSTORM
In this exercise, we are looking at the bigger picture. What are the major obstacles and challenges that must be overcome to transition from your current growth performance level to your target level?

EXERCISE 2.3
1.   Think about your most critical SMART objectives.

2.   On a new page in your planning document or spreadsheet, create three columns. At the top of the right hand column, write a short description of the target state for that objective. For example, using the SMART objective from Exercise 1.4, the target state is $10 million in annualized contract value, 20 new customers, and so on. At the bottom of the left hand column, write your current performance level for that same objective. For instance, your current performance may be $9 million from 18 new customers.

3.   Now, brainstorm all of the potential problems, challenges and obstacles in your path from getting to your current performance level to your target performance level. Write those down in the middle column. Be sure to consider all of the implications and unintended consequences getting to the target state will have on your organization (customers, customer service, human resources, operations, etc.). Repeat this step of the process for each of your SMART objectives.

4.   Next, without revealing the middle column, share the page with a buddy or advisor and ask them what to brainstorm what they perceive to be problems, challenges, and obstacles in your path. Don't worry about solving these issues yet. (You may also conduct part 6 of this exercise with a group.)

5.   Add any new challenges from your buddy or team's list and it to your sheet.

6.   Should any of these new issues become SMART objectives? How does this new information change the priority of your current SMART objectives list?

EXERCISE 2.4 DRAFT

After completing exercises 2.1 through 2.3 you now have the information you need to draft the "gap analysis" and "current situation" section of your strategic plan. Most plan writers brush this section off and give it short shrift. While it is not long, it is a critically important summary of your business state.

EXERCISE 2.4

1. Keep it short. Draft 1-2 paragraphs summarizing the findings of your quick audit and performance levels.

2. Add another 1-2 paragraphs explaining your current performance levels including the basic data (number of customers, sales, etc.) as well as the major reasons why performance is strong or weak.

3. Finalize the section by adding a short summary of the Gap Analysis, highlighting the major challenges that must be addressed in order to accomplish your objectives.

4. Don't forget to update the Objectives section of the plan based on the findings from the exercises in Chapter 2.

⌘

CHAPTER 2. RESOURCES

RECOMMENDED AUDIT CHART DATA POINTS (MARKETING)

- Google AdWords (SEM) & Online ads
  - Impressions (all campaigns)
  - Clicks (all campaigns)
  - Click Through Rate (all campaigns)
  - Cost Per Click (average across all campaigns)
  - Average Position
  - Conversion Rate (clicks/calls and forms)
  - Web Form completions
  - Successful phone calls

- Organic Website Traffic
  - Total Sessions
  - Users
  - Page views
  - Pages/Visit
  - % New Visits
  - Returning Visits
  - Average Time on Site
  - Bounce Rate
  - Direct Traffic %
  - Referral %
  - Social %
  - Email %
  - Search Traffic %
  - Top Referring Sites

- Public Relations
  - Speaking Engagements
  - Interviews
  - Article Placements
  - Reach/Impressions

- Social Media
  - Connections
  - Posts
  - Impressions
  - Links To Site
  - Followers

- E-blasts
  - Number of Blasts Sent
  - Total Recipients
  - Opens
  - Open Rate
  - Clicks
  - CTR
  - Bounces
  - Opt-outs
  - Replies
    - Incoming Calls
    - Landing page visits/conversions

- Direct Mail
  - Quantity sent
  - Incoming Calls
  - Landing page visits

- Trade Shows/Events
  - Number of Exhibitions
  - Total Attendees
  - Pre-Mailers
  - Post Show Mailers / E-mails
  - Quantity of Mailers (contacts)
  - Pre-Event Meeting Calls
  - Business Cards Collected (prospects)
  - Landing page visits/conversions

OTHER PERFORMANCE AUDIT AREAS FOR REVIEW
- Current marketing plan. Do you have one? Is it effective?
- Marketing team. How well do they perform?
- Current sales plan. Do you have one? Is it effective?
- Sales team. How well do they perform?
- Creative review. Is your creative marketing material effective?
- Agency review. Is your ad agency or marketing firm up to par?
- Affiliates / partners / alliances
- Forecast. How accurate is your forecast?
- Marketing / sales alignment. Are your sales and marketing team in alignment or is there friction?
- Budget. What is your budgeting process and do your leaders proactively manage their department budgets?

RECOMMENDED READING

Data Driven Marketing, Jeffery, Mark, 2010.

First Things Fast, Rossett, Allison, 2009.

The Marketing Audit, Skelton, Orlando, 2015.

The Marketing Audit Handbook, Malherbe, Dawid, 2012.

Marketing Metrics, Bendle, Farris, Pfeifer, Reibstein, 2015.

Sales Audit, Hutchison, Corey, 2007.

Unleashing the Power of PR, Weiner, Mark, 2006.

3 CUSTOMER ANALYSIS

Curious things, habits. People themselves never knew they had them.
-Agatha Christie

H OW WELL do you really know your customers? The truth is, you can never know them well enough. But, you just may be able to know them even better than they know themselves. For sure, the best growth strategies are based on a keen understanding of what customers really want and creating a delivery system to give it to them better than anyone else (at every stage of the customer relationship). Always remember this: no matter what you are selling, it's not what the customer is really buying. Your customers are buying the benefit that they get from the thing they buy. Where it gets tricky is the benefit they want is tied to a weird brew of emotions, memories, history, tradition, culture, prejudices, rationalizations, politics, commitments, and number of other psycho-socials factors. Your job is to filter through the muck to find a kernel of truth in order to consistently make the sale.

CHAPTER 3 OBJECTIVES
By the close of Session 3, you will develop a set of strategic tools that you can use to find and then apply your customer truths, including:
- Customer profiles and personas
- Buyer decision maps, trigger motivators, and corresponding selling maps
- Paths to reach your customers

EXERCISE 3.1 RESEARCH
TARGET CUSTOMER DEMOGRAPHICS
Start with the basics facts about your customers. Do you have your customers' latest demographic data at your fingertips? If not, it doesn't take long to build a relatively accurate statistical profile. This is important for both b2c and b2b business models.

EXERCISE 3.1 YOUR CUSTOMER PROFILE
1. Build a base level demographic snapshot of your current customer base. Include the following information:
    - Age
    - Gender
    - Race
    - Education
    - Income
    - Location

2. Now, segment your customer base by adding in additional factors relevant to your business (e.g., decision-makers, product or service types, or other classifications). If you have the date, go as granular as you can with the information. For instance, For B2B models, you should also factor in business classifications such as industry types, size (revenue, employees), etc. Further segmentation like customer's values and life stage may also prove helpful. Also consider their pleasures, vices, habits and other preferences.

3. Review the data. Are patterns emerging? Are there concentrations of customer populations that you serve more than others? Are there underserved populations that are potential markets for you?

4. If there are target customers that are not being served, build basic demographic profiles for those market segments as well.

5. Conduct a quick Internet search for some of the latest research findings about your current customers. Look for any insights and trends that help you better understand your customer base. Set up Google alerts for your current customers and prospects.

6. Conduct a search of the US Statistical Abstract for your customer profiles. You can also check your economic development boards and chambers for additional statistical data. Using this information, roughly calculate your share of market for each of your target

segments. Why? Your share of market lets you know how much more growth is available and how well you are doing.

EXERCISE 3.2 FOCUS
WHAT DO YOUR CUSTOMERS REALLY BUY?
No matter what you are selling, the tangible goods of your product or service are not what your customers are buying. Your customers are buying the intangible benefits derived from your product or service. Often, those benefits are psychological and emotional.
All buyers make irrational choices and then rationalize their decisions. And most don't know they are doing it. (This is true in all industries.)

EXERCISE 3.2
1.   Fill in the blanks:
     • My target audience is a _____.
     • His state of mind is _____.
     • He thinks he needs _____.
     • He really wants _____.
     • But he will settle for _____.
     • He wants to feel _____.
     • He really needs _____.

2.   What is the main benefit your customer is looking for?

3.   Think about a recent purchase you made. How would you answer the questions above about yourself as you made the purchase?

4.   Now, think about your business and how well you provide what your customer really wants and how you make him feel. How do the benefits you provide match his wants and the way he wants to feel? How can you improve?

5.   Now, complete the table below, considering the problem or challenge that your customer is trying to solve:

Table 1. CUSTOMER PAIN POINTS

Challenge / Problem: *The obstacles and roadblocks in the path to getting what they want*	
Current Solution: *What are they doing now to solve the problem?*	
Pain Points (if unsolved): *What is happening as a result of the unsolved challenge?*	
Pain Points (if unsolved): *What is happening as a result of the unsolved challenge?*	
Need / Requirements: *A description of what the solution looks like and any specific conditions*	
Perceived Needs (Wants): *What are the irrational, often emotional demands of the decision-maker?*	
Objections: *Why the decision-maker thinks/feels/believes the solution won't work*	
Motivators: *The basic drivers that prompt the decision-maker to act now*	

EXERCISE 3.3 RESEARCH
CUSTOMER BUYING DECISION MAP

Understanding the process your customers follow when buying your product or service will help you identify not only when they are most receptive to your marketing and sales efforts, you will also be able to customize your own process to increase your likelihood of success. Mapping this process will help shape your own marketing & sales funnel.

EXERCISE 3.3

1. Identify the major steps in your customer's buying process. Typically, most customers follow a predictable path (even if they don't realize it). See the sample decision map at the end of this chapter and adapt it for your customer. (You may need multiple decision paths depending on your customer segment or product type.) Some are very short with minimal steps. Others may take years with multiple, complex steps.

2. Where do your customers typically get held up in the process?

3. How long does each step of the decision process generally take?

4. How can you help your customers navigate their own decision map?

5. How can you accelerate the decision-making process?

EXERCISE 3.4 RESEARCH
LIFE PATTERNS
Buy decisions are made by real people who follow patterns of behaviors. These behaviors develop into life patterns. This information can be mined to help you identify both marketing (general behavioral patterns) and sales opportunities (specific behaviors of target individuals).

EXERCISE 3.4
1. What are the typical daily routines of your customers? For instance, consider how their days are spent:
    a. Daily (home, commute, work, lunch/errands, commute, home, dinner, relaxation/recreation, sleep).
    b. Weekend (home, errands, fun, family, worship)

2. When are these patterns disrupted? (e.g., job changes, sickness, death, vacation, marital status, life stage change, children)

3. Identify relevant specific patterns for your customer (e.g., what is their daily work routine?)

4. Identify the ways your customers become distracted (e.g., fantasy, humor, sex, world events)?

5. What are the best points to intercept your customer during their routines? When are they most receptive? Where will you intercept them? How will you intercept? (Generally, buyers are most receptive during their search stage.)

6. Is your product or service a part of their work or life pattern or are you a disruption? Are you a welcome distraction?

7. Are there opportunities to further segment your customers?

8. Conduct another Internet search to find reliable research insights on these customer segments.

9. Apply these findings to your customer analysis.

EXERCISE 3.5 BRAINSTORM
CUSTOMER PERSONAS
Bring your data and demographic profiles to life. Construct a persona for each of your target customer types. The more detail, the better. You can base them on real-life customers. Use the persona to help make customer-facing decisions.

EXERCISE 3.5
1. Conduct a small team brainstorming session with creative team members who understand your customers well.
2. Pick a name for your customer persona.
3. Construct a virtual life for your persona covering the following elements:
    - Where do he live? House, apartment, rent, own?
    - How many household members? Children?
    - What are his breakfast, lunch, and dinner habits and favorites?
    - Where does he shop? For groceries, clothes, stuff?
    - What are his favorite clothing brands?
    - What kind of car (make, model) does he drive?
    - What are his tastes in music and favorite and music channels?
    - What are his favorite TV shows and networks (Cable, DIRECTV, Internet, etc.?)?
    - What are his favorite sports and teams?
    - What are his favorite drinks? Favorite brand?
    - What is his favorite restaurant?
    - What is he reading – which magazines, or books?
    - Where does he get them (e.g., bookstore, subscriptions, library)?
    - What are his socials media habits and preferred platforms?
    - Where does he go on vacation?
    - What is his proudest accomplishment?
    - What is his biggest hope or dream?
    - What's on his bucket list?
    - What are his hobbies?
    - Is he religious? What is his faith? Where does he worship?
    - Where did he grow up?
    - What are his pet peeves?
    - What is his biggest regret or disappointment?

EXERCISE 3.6 DRAFT

Briefly, but including all relevant detail draft a summary of your findings in exercise 3.1-3.5. Make sure to include all data charts and tables, explaining key customer insights and customer behaviors impact your business. Also include the summarized results of any primary customer research conducted and reference 3rd party research sources.

EXERCISE 3.6

1. Create a new section in your growth plan document file, titled "Market Analysis".
2. Make sure to address the following basic questions:
    - Which market segments are the most attractive? Why?
    - What channels exist to reach the segment?
    - Where are the best places to reach the most of them?
    - What potential channels can be created to reach the segment?
    - What products or services are the best matches for the needs of the target customer?
    - When is the best time to reach a target customer (time of year? time of month? time of week? time of day?)?
3. Don't jump to conclusions just yet. At this stage of the plan, our aim is to take away insights. We will determine how we will apply them later. There may be key questions to which you do not yet have an answer. At this point, that is OK. However, additional customer research may be required to find those answers.
4. Make sure to earmark funds in your budget to complete the research and then update your strategy and plan.

⌘

CHAPTER 3. RESOURCES

BUYER DECISION PROCESS STEPS

1. Pain point (e.g., emotional, physical, financial, temporal)
2. Problem assessment
3. Search for answers
4. Identification of potential solutions
5. Search for solution providers
6. Referral request
7. Long list of possible solution providers
8. Disqualification of providers, round 1
9. Short list of solution providers
10. Disqualification of providers, round 2
11. Contact / Inquiry providers
12. RFQ issued to providers
13. Proposal review
14. Disqualification of providers, round 3
15. Presentation by providers
16. Disqualification of providers, round 4
17. Committee review
18. Contract review
19. Negotiation of terms
20. Selection of provider
21. Use & evaluation of providers product
22. Disposal of product solution

RECOMMENDED READING

Buyer Personas, Revella, Adele, 2014.

Buyology, Lindstrom, Martin, 2008.

Decoding The New Consumer Mind, Yarrow, Kit, 2014.

Influence: The Psychology of Persuasion, Cialdini, Robert B., PhD. 2009.

Positioning, Trout & Reis, 1981.

Predictably Irrational, Ariely, Dan 2009.

Ogilvy On Advertising, Ogilvy, David, 1983

Why We Buy: The Science of Shopping, Underhill, Paco, 2000.

4 COMPETITIVE ANALYSIS

In accordance with our principles of free enterprise and healthy competition, I am going to ask you two to fight to the death for it. -Monty Python

WOULDN'T IT be great if you were a monopoly and all customers had to buy from you? (OK, that really wouldn't be a good thing for a lot of reasons. But, it would make things a lot easier.) The fact is we're not alone out there. There are a whole lot of competitors just waiting in the wings to swoop in and eat your lunch. No need to become paranoid. You can use your competitors to make you even stronger. And, your competitors will actually help you shape your growth strategy. How? Think of it this way, your competitors have done a lot of the heavy lifting for you. What can you learn from them? Analyzing your competitors' strengths and weaknesses will reveal openings in the market that you can use to your advantage.

CHAPTER 4. OBJECTIVES
By the end of Chapter 4, you will better understand your industry, your competitors and your own strengths and weaknesses, through:
- Industry analysis
- Competitive analysis
- SWOT assessments

This information can be used to identify openings in the market that will provide a crack to pry open or a toehold to secure your strategic footing.

EXERCISE 4.1 RESEARCH
INDUSTRY ANALYSIS
The most important part of this is exercise to identify and monitor trends that will impact your business. The key insights are how these trends in the industry will impact your customer.

EXERCISE 4.1
1. Market Overview
   - How big is your industry? (Nationally, Regionally, Locally)
   - Is it expanding or shrinking
   - How is the industry typically segmented? (e.g., size, type/specialization, customer focus)
   - Is the industry part of a bigger industry tier (e.g., financial services, defense, agriculture)?
   - Where is your business in the big picture?

2. How Does The Industry Work?
   - How does the industry serve its customer base?
   - How has that changed recently? How will it likely change in the future?
   - What are the major links in the value chain (from end-user through to suppliers)?
   - How does the supply chain work?
   - Who are the major providers / players in the space? Who are the clear leaders? Why?
   - Is that changing? Who are the game changers?
   - What drives the industry? (Price? Service? Tech innovations?)

3. Major Trends
   - What is happening in the industry that will likely impact your business (i.e., helps or hinders your ability to meet your objectives)?
   - Is the industry thriving or dying? Why?
   - Is it stable or fragile?
   - What stage is the industry in (infancy, mature)?
   - What is trending in your business right now (new government regulations, changes in technology, consolidation, increase / decrease in investment, increase in the number of players (competitors, suppliers)?
   - Identify potential major disruptions. What developments could outright crush your business? Is that likely to happen? What are the warning signs?

4. So What?

- How is the industry data relevant to your business and the growth strategy?
- Which of the trends are threats or opportunities (for your and your customers)?
- How are they threats? What level (high, low)?
- How are they opportunities? What is the value of the opportunity and how do you measure it?
- How will this change your business?
  - Does it make it easier or harder and how?
  - How does it effect pricing?
  - How will it impact your bottom line and top line?
- Keep a running tab on these issues and update your report frequently (at least quarterly) and share it with your team.

EXERCISE 4.2 RESEARCH
COMPETITIVE ANALYSIS
Construct a survey of the competitive landscape and build profiles of your major competitors. The most important information is how your competitors are serving your shared customer base and how you can capitalize on their weaknesses or mitigate threats.

EXERCISE 4.2 SIZE UP THE COMPETITION
1. Identify Your Competition
   - Direct competitors (by type or class)
   - Adjacent players
   - Market share (by customer? revenue? product type? – whatever measure is most important to you)

2. Profile Your Competitors
   - Size (Revenue, employees, locations)
   - Locations (market heat maps)
   - Product and service offerings / features & benefits
   - Value platform / marketing positioning
   - Key differentiators / competitive advantages
   - Sales & marketing strategy and tactics?
   - Pricing / Fees
   - Profit / employee

3. Conduct a Competitive SWOT Review (for each major competitor)
   - What are their strengths? / What do you need to guard against?
   - Of the critical target audience factors, which competitors meet the customers' needs/wants best?
   - What are their weaknesses? / How can you beat them?
   - How are they threatening your business?
   - What are the opportunities that allow you to take advantage of their weaknesses?

4. How Do You Stack Up?
   - Devise a grading system to rank yourself and other players (e.g., numerical rankings 1-5; or "strong / weak") using the most important analysis factors.
   - Based on your review and scoring, where are the marketing openings and opportunities?

EXERCISE 4.3 FOCUS & BRAINSTORM
SWOT ANALYSIS
Conduct a simple SWOT analysis session with your trusted team. Brainstorm how you can block, tackle and attack your competitors and create more value for your customers. Solicit feedback from your team, and complete the following questions. Use the table at the end of the chapter. Remember to keep your customer in mind – how well is your organization meeting their wants and needs?

EXERCISE 4.3
1. Strengths
    • What do we do really well?
    • What is the one thing we are BEST at?
    • Last year, _____ worked great.
    • Customers really like the way we _____.

2. Weaknesses
    • Did we accomplish our strategic objectives last year? Why or Why not?
    • What did NOT work well last year?
    • What is the one thing we are WORST at?
    • If we only had _____, we would be great!
    • If we only knew _____, we would be great!
    • If only there was more _____.
    • If only there was less_____.

3. Opportunities
    • I am really excited about _____.
    • _____ is the best thing since sliced bread.
    • Customers really seem to like _____.
    • Other businesses, like _____ tried _____ and it worked!

4. Threats
    • I am really concerned about _____.
    • If _____ happens, we are sunk!
    • A lot of customers complain about _____.
    • Customers seem interested in Competitor X's _____.

5. Solutions
    • If you fired yourself today, and came back tomorrow as a new boss

with a clean sheet, what would you do differently based on this SWOT?

- Brainstorm at least 3 ways each you can mitigate weaknesses, block threats, attack opportunities, and leverage your strengths to better serve your customers and outperform your competition.
- Does this information change your SMART objectives? If so, how? Make sure to update them.

EXERCISE 4.4 DRAFT

Package up your work from exercise 4.1-4.3 and add it to the market analysis section of your growth plan.

EXERCISE 4.4 COMPLETE THE MARKET ANALYSIS
1. Draft a short summary introduction and summary paragraph for each of the 3 exercises in session 4.
2. Be sure to include all tables and charts.
3. Call out major insights and opportunities.

Review your SMART Objectives and update them based on the work in exercise 4. Make any necessary changes in priority. Make objectives more specific if possible based on the new insights.

⌘

CHAPTER 4 RESOURCES

Table 2. SWOT TABLE

Strengths:	*How will we leverage our strengths?*
Weakness:	*How will mitigate weakness?*
Opportunities:	*How will we attack opportunities?*
Threats:	*How will we block threats?*

RECOMMENDED READING

Business & Competitive Analysis, Fleisher, Craig, Bensoussan, Babette, 2007.

Competitive Strategy, Porter, Michael, 1980.

Early Warning, Gilad, Ben, PhD., 2003.

5 YOUR STRATEGY: WHY BUY FROM YOU?

Choices are made in brief seconds, and paid for in the time that remains.
-Paolo Giordano

"WHY SHOULD I buy from you rather than someone else?"

Customers ask that question in a lot of different ways. Be grateful they are asking. It is an important part of your customer conversation. But, you better have a good answer. A good answer is crafted in your business and brand value platform, your USP and competitive advantage. Before you give an answer, make sure they ask the question first. To do that, you'll need to make sure you found the best way to get the conversation started. There's lots of ways to do it. So, you'll want to choose wisely. On a larger scale, you also need to apply what you've learned so far and begin to formulate your growth strategy. By now, you probably can see interesting answers to your SMART Objective challenge questions. Are there strategies that answer your customers' question and your challenge question?

CHAPTER 5 OBJECTIVES
By the end of Session 5, you will have some new tools to help you evaluate market opportunities and make stronger strategic decisions. You will also craft your:
- Business value platform
- Unique selling proposition
- Competitive advantage

EXERCISE 5.1 ANALYSIS & BRAINSTORM
IDENTIFY MARKET OPENINGS
Your work to date has produced a lot of information about your customers, your market and your competition. Now's the time to carefully examine those findings and look for openings in the market for you to make a play. This exercise will form the beginning shape of your strategy.

EXERCISE 5.1
1. Examine the findings from your customer & SWOT analysis. Are there better ways to deliver what your customers need and want?

2. Are there new or adjacent markets that can be tapped?

3. Now review your competitive analysis. Are there areas where they are under serving the customer base?

4. Are there attractive markets being served by your competitors that you have not penetrated?

5. Capture all of the potential market openings in a document. Then, hold a brainstorming session with your team. Share your list of market openings and challenge your team to identify at lest 10 more openings. (Don't analyze or disqualify any ideas yet or worry about HOW you will attack the opening. Strive for as many potential openings as possible).

6. Then, review the big list of market openings and ask: "If we seized this opening, would it help accomplish our primary SMART Objectives?"

7. Save all of the openings where you answered "Yes" to #6 above for the next exercise.

EXERCISE 5.2 BRAINSTORM & QUESTION
IDENTIFY STRATEGIC OPTIONS

Remember the challenge questions you crafted for your smart objectives? It is time to use them. You'll pair them with the market openings from exercise 5.1 and brainstorm answers to each of the challenge questions. You will also develop a list of criteria that can be used to evaluate your ideas and determine which options are the best.

EXERCISE 5.2

1. Create a new page with a 3-columned table. In the left hand column, insert the challenge questions based on your SMART objectives. In the middle column, insert each of the marketing openings from 5.1. Leave the right-hand column blank for now.

2. Regroup with your team and conduct a brainstorm session to generate as many answers to the challenge questions as possible. In the session, encourage the use of the "What if...?" question. That is, when an idea is presented to solve the "How will we accomplish our objective?" challenge question, phrase the idea as follows:

   "What if we tried this idea?"

   This phrasing creates a more positive session experience and will likely produce more ideas. Or, back to the challenge question example from Chapter 1, a potential solution might be:

   "What if we recruited our biggest competitor's best sales leader?"

   Build on ideas and refrain from discarding them now. Again, strive for a large number of ideas because you will evaluate them later. The goal is to make sure you leave no stone unturned. Ideally, you will be able to easily map each of the answers directly to a market opening. These answers may be big picture strategies or they may be tactical. Capture them all. Be bold. Be creative.

3. Next, brainstorm of list of critical factors that you will use to evaluate your potential opportunity answers. Don't apply any of the factors yet or disqualify any ideas. The goal is to simply develop a list of criteria by which you will measure the strength of the potential opportunities. In general, most organizations consider several factors, such as:
   - Effectiveness (will the idea actually produce the intended results?)
   - Revenue potential (how much additional revenue will the idea generate if implemented?)

- Cost (how much capital is required to execute the idea?)
- Timing (how long will it take to execute the idea and generate results?)
- Labor requirements (do you need additional staff? Do you have the right talent to execute the idea?)
- Competitive advantage (will the idea leverage your competitive advantage? Will it create another competitive advantage?)

4. Once you have your list of criteria, establish a simple rating scale for each factor (the simpler, the better). See the sample evaluation matrix at the end of this chapter.

5. Think about your options and how you will evaluate them for a week, several days at minimum.

6. Now, buddy up and share your scored options with your advisor for his or her opinion.

7. Based on feedback, you may need to adjust your evaluation system, scoring framework or criteria.

EXERCISE 5.3 FOCUS, ROLE PLAY & HOLE PUNCH
BVP, USP, COMPETITIVE ADVANTAGES & PROOF POINTS

While your strategic opportunities are marinating, it is time to start crafting four important strategic constructs that will help focus your strategy: your business value platform, unique selling proposition, competitive advantages and proof points. These tools help ensure that whichever strategic direction you go, you will stay on target.

EXERCISE 5.3

1. Answer the following questions:

   • Why should I do business with you, instead of any and every other option available to me, including the option of doing nothing at all?

   • What are three things you want your customers to know about your business? (Will these things eliminate my pain point and give me what I want?)

   • How do you deliver those three most important things to your customer?

   • If your customers need _____, how do you get it to them better than anybody else?

   • Is anyone better than you at what you do?

   • What are your core competencies?

   • What are you committed to providing your customers?

   • What can your company promise?

2. Capture your answers in a short paragraph.

3. Next, construct a simple table or spreadsheet with three columns. In the left hand column, name or briefly describe your primary products and key features of each product. Then, in the middle column, define the effect or result of each of the product or service features. Finally, in the right-hand column, define the benefit the customer derives from this feature. Do the benefits for the customers match what the customers really buy from Exercise 3.2? If so, you are in good shape. If not, you will need to reevaluate which of your products and features are

relevant to your customers.

4. Draft your Unique Selling Proposition (USP). First, answer the following questions as if you were your customer:
   - Why should I read or listen to you?
   - Why should I believe what you have to say?
   - Why should I do anything about what you offer?
   - Why should I act now?

5. Then, using these answers and elements of your BVP, craft a response to those questions in a single sentence. This is your USP.

6. Now, test your BVP and USP in a short role-play session with a buddy or advisor. Pretend your buddy is a potential customer who asks, "How can you help me?" Your USP answer should include the following elements:
   - Here's who we are.
   - Here's what we've got for you.
   - Here's what it will do for you.
   - Here's what to do now.

7. How did your buddy react? How will you refine your USP based on your buddy's reaction and feedback? Here's a fill in the blank approach (developed by Perry Marshall's Ultimate Guide To Google AdWords that works really well):

   My company helps [this group of people]... do or get [this benefit]...even if [worst-case believable scenario.]

8. Think about your USP, your BVP and the features and benefits you provide. Answer these two questions:
   - How are you able to provide these features and benefits better than anybody else?
   - What is uniquely different about your delivery system?

   The answers to these questions form the basis of your competitive advantage. It is important to point out that while your competitive advantages are about your business, they are ultimately about how you better serve your customers.

9. Next, add a column to the right of the table you created in 5.2. Next to each of the benefits, insert the corresponding competitive advantage.

(It is OK if more than one benefit is derived from the same competitive advantage.) Remember, the benefit is the value that you create for your customer.

10. Develop a set of claims backing up your BENEFIT/RESULTS for customers (but, not your features!) These claims should quantifiable and measurable. And, all claims must be supported by demonstrable evidence. Think of it this way: imagine a potential customer demands, "Prove it!" when you mention a particular benefit.
    - How would you prove it to him?
    - What would serve as verifiable evidence?
    - Brainstorm compelling proof points for each benefit and add them to your table.

11. Share your Features/Benefits/Advantages/Proof Point table with a buddy. Ask him or her to Hole Punch your proof points. How can you make the proof points more compelling?

12. Now return to your running list of strategic options and your evaluation criteria. Separately or as a group, ask each team member to numerically score each of the strategic options ideas using the rating factors devised above. Take your time and discuss each score in depth.

13. What are your top scoring strategic options? What do these top-scoring options share in common? Do they represent a single strategic play or are they multiple strategies? Consider the following overarching strategies commonly deployed. Do your strategic options fall into one of these strategy categories? Of course, this is not an exhaustive list, merely some suggestions to get you thinking about how to change up your game:
    - First mover. Lead the pack with a new product or service or create an entirely new category
    - M&A. Join forces and grow rapidly
    - Diversify. Enter a new product or service category, spread risk and create cross sell opportunities
    - Consolidate. Shed unattractive business lines and focus on core competencies
    - Reorganize. Streamline or expand departments or team structures
    - Refinance. Reorganize your debt or equity ideals to improve your capital position
    - Close.
    - Expand. Add more market locations, franchise or establish a chain

- Change quality (high or low). Improve quality or offer value package options
- Change speed. Accelerate the cycle of solutions or slow it down with enhanced experience levels
- Service. Develop a high touch or low touch experience options
- Innovation. Develop a new or improved product or service in your category
- New market vertical. Provide the same products or services in a different industry.
- Sell more to current customer base. Up sell or cross sell
- Sell same to more customers in same vertical.
- Attrition. Ride out tough economies or crowded fields and outlast your competitor
- Price flux. Lower or raise prices
- Control supply chain. Negotiate better deals with suppliers, vertically integrate

14. Once your options have been thoroughly vetted, some clear winners will start to emerge. Which combinations of your options form the most compelling answer? This is where the magic happens. As you continue to methodically identify and evaluate options (both strategic and tactical), you are formulating your overall growth strategy. In simple terms, your strategy is the highest scoring set of answers to your challenge question.

You don't need to commit to any given strategy just yet. You are still in the planning phase. But, at least you have some clear winning options. The next three chapter exercises will help you determine which strategy to execute.

EXERCISE 5.4 DRAFT

The high scoring strategic options may form the basis for your overall strategy. Before you commit and make a final strategic decision, create a draft of the strategy section of your plan to try it on for size. Before you commit, at least commit it to paper.

EXERCISE 5.4

1. Draft a short summary intro and summary paragraph for each of the 3 exercises in Chapter 5.

2. Draft a short paragraph describing how your top scoring opportunities for a coherent strategy. Be sure that the proposed strategy clearly answers how you will achieve all of your SMART your objectives.

3. Include your Business Value Platform, Unique Selling Proposition, and Feature/Benefits tables.

4. What other companies (not in your industry) are executing or have executed similar strategies? If they succeeded, why were they successful? How can you replicate their success in your strategy? If they did not succeed, why? How will you learn from their mistakes? Include these answers in your strategy summary.

⌘

CHAPTER 5. RESOURCES

Table 3. SAMPLE FEATURES/BENEFIT TABLE

Product / Service Feature:	*What aspects of your product or service are unique or different you're your competition?*
Feature Effect:	*What impact or result is derived from this feature?*
Customer Benefit:	*How does this make your customer's life better?*
Competitive Advantage:	*Do you improve your customer's life better than your competitor?*
Proof Point:	*How will you prove your claims?*

RECOMMENDED READING

Creating Competitive Advantage, Jaynie Smith, 2006.

Competitive Advantage, Porter, Michael, 1998.

The Decision Book: 50 Models for Strategic Thinking, Krogerus, Mikael &
Tschäppeler, Roman, 2012.

E-Myth Revisited, Gerber, Michael, 2009.

The End of Competitive Advantage, McGrath, Rita, 2013.

The Innovators Hypothesis, Schrage, Michael, 2014.

Making Hard Decisions, Clemens, Robert, 1997.

Smart Choices, Hammond, Keeney, Raifa, 2002.

Value Prop, Palomino, Jose, 2008.

Value Proposition Design, Osterwalder, Alexander, 2015.

6 YOUR BUYER'S JOURNEY FUNNEL

You can get everything in life you want, if you help enough other people get what they want. -Zig Ziglar

THE BUYER'S Journey Funnel has its flaws. But, as a strategic construct, it is an incredibly powerful and practical planning tool. As you continue to evaluate your strategic options, the Buyer's Journey Funnel helps you calculate the impact, effect and implications of a strategic option.

CHAPTER 6 OBJECTIVES
By the end of Chapter 6, you will:
• Craft a Buyer's Journey Funnel model for your growth strategy
• Define Key Performance Indicators, the buyer behavioral and performance triggers that signal success

EXERCISE 6.1 FOCUS
FINALIZE BUYING DECISION MAP & SALES PROCESS
To make the customer journey funnel work for you, build it from the ground up and based on your customers' decision process. Tailor your sales process to make it easy to buy from you.

EXERCISE 6.1

1. Update the Customer Buying Decision Map from Exercise 3.3 capturing any additional customer insights from the past 3 exercises. How can you make their decision process easier?

2. Now, review your current sales process to make sure that you can effectively and efficiently match your sales process to the customers' decision map. In a new document or spreadsheet, put the steps of the buyer's decision process in one column and your selling process in the next column. (Note: for most organizations, the selling process begins with a qualified lead. The marketing process generates those qualified leads.)

3. Are there steps in your process that should be improved to make the buying experience easier for your customers? Are there any unnecessary steps that can be eliminated? How would you revise your selling process to better match the customer's buy process? How can you make the process move faster? Which steps of the selling process could be automated? Which steps require the hands on labor of your sales team?

4. Next, turn your attention to your current marketing process. Typically, this process is designed around generating leads for your sales team. Add these steps to your spreadsheet in the same column but right above your sales process steps divided by a line.

5. How well does your current marketing process map to your customer's buying decision process? Are there any customer decision steps left open or unaccounted for? If so, brainstorm how your marketing will fill those gaps. You may need to create a marketing campaign specifically for each of these buyer decision steps.

EXERCISE 6.2 ANALYSIS & BRAINSTORM
KEY PERFORMANCE INDICATORS

Carefully review the steps from exercise 6.1. And the results of your marketing performance analysis in exercise 2. Which of the steps in the process are you most effective? Which steps are powerful catalysts for moving prospective customers through their decision process? In other words, which are the critical steps that advance the buyer toward a sale. These are your KPI's.

EXERCISE 6.2

1. Take a close look at your updated process steps from Exercise 6.1 and compare it to your marketing past performance.

    •   Identify steps where the process stalls or stops. How many and what percentage of your leads are dying here at these steps? Is that acceptable? What can you do better here?

    •   Identify steps where you are especially effective at converting to the next step or springboard steps that leapfrog over other steps and result in a closed sale. How many and what percentage of your closed sales come from this step? What can you do to make these initiatives a best practice?

2. Brainstorm (alone or with a group) the reasons why the process stalls or stops at the steps from 1a above. (Note: often, prospects will disqualify themselves at these points. That's ok as long as you can learn and refine your target customer profile based on the information. That way, you aren't wasting money and time attracting these customer segments into the process.)

3. Brainstorm the reasons why the steps from 1b are highly effective. Why do you perform so well at this step?

4. What other steps in the process are critical to converting to a sale?

NOTE: These critical steps are likely your Key Performance Indicators. That is, the results in these steps are likely predictors of the health of both individual sales and the health of your overall process. KPI's need to be carefully monitored and measured. In addition, your marketing should drive prospects to these steps to most effectively advance the sale.

EXERCISE 6.3 FOCUS
BUILD YOUR CUSTOMER JOURNEY FUNNEL
The buyer journey funnel (or customer journey funnel) is a benchmark strategic construct and an enormously helpful and practical planning tool. We'll draft a traditional version and then customize it to meet your business model. Growing your business is a numbers game. The funnel helps you calculate what those numbers need to be for you to succeed.

EXERCISE 6.3

1. Using the example at the end of this chapter, create a copy in a spreadsheet or table. (A spreadsheet program like Excel that allows you to create formulas is helpful.)

2. In the left hand column, create the typical journey funnel segments from Awareness/Discovery to Engagement to Nurture to Prime and then Close. (It won't look like a funnel just yet. That's ok.)

3. Then, in another adjacent column, insert the appropriate steps from your customers' buying decision process map under each of the segment headers. Does each of the steps have a matching category segment? Is anything missing? If so, you may need to add or delete segments from the column as needed.

4. Next, create another column next to the funnel segments. Insert the appropriate and matching steps from the updated marketing and sales processes next to the corresponding funnel segments. Add another column in your spreadsheet to the right and label it "Conversion Rate".

5. Then, if you have the data from your marketing performance analysis, plug in your performance data starting with closed sales and working your way back up the funnel. If you know your average conversion rates, plug those numbers in as well.

NOTE: You may need to do this for each product lines or customer segments if they do not follow the same funnel patterns. You may also need to create funnels for each campaign that you run.

6. Plug in your target objectives. Based on your current conversion rates, how wide does the top of your funnel need to be in order to generate the sales activity you need? That is, how may hits do you need to make the rest of the numbers work in order to reach your target objective?

Play around with different conversion rates and factors, keeping a close eye on those key performance indicators steps. Think about how you will manage lost leads and recycling leads through the funnel. The funnel can also be used as a tracking tool. Once you launch your marketing or sales campaign, you will be able to gauge your progress and measure your actual performance against your performance targets. The funnel will show you precisely at which stage you are on or off target. So, you know what you need to change.

⌘

CHAPTER 6. RESOURCES

Table 5. YOUR JOURNEY FUNNEL TABLE

Stage	Target	Target %	Actual	Actual %	Date	KPI	Key Message	Call To Action	Cost
Awareness									
Engage									
Nurture									
Prime									
Close									

RECOMMENDED READING

80/20 Sales & Marketing, Marshall, Perry, 2013.

The Funnel Principle, Sellers, Mark, 2010.

Sales & Marketing the Six Sigma Way, Webb, Michael J. 2013.

7 YOUR INTEGRATED TACTICAL PLAN

I get up every morning determined to both change the world and have one hell of a good time. Sometimes this makes planning my day difficult. -E.B. White

YOUR STRATEGY is becoming more fine-tuned. But, how are you going to execute the strategy to achieve your SMART Objectives? Now, you need a tactical plan and a team that can pull it off. That means more options need to be evaluated and decisions must be made.

CHAPTER 7. OBJECTIVES
By the end of Chapter 7, you will:
• Explore and evaluate tactical options
• Build a tactical execution plan for your strategies
• Draft a team to help do it

• EXERCISE 7.1 BRAINSTORMING

TACTICAL SUPPORT FOR YOUR STRATEGY

Your strategy is forming. You've identified several options and are closing in on one or a combination of options. Now you need to define how you are going to execute your strategy. Your funnel provides lots of clues. But you have to figure out how you are going to make the strategy work.

EXERCISE 7.1

1. Bring in a team of trusted creative thinkers and conduct a brainstorming session. Share your work to date, your SMART objectives and the highlights of your strategy. Task the team to generate as many ideas on how to execute your strategy as possible. Capture all of the ideas and don't worry about any constraints. Let the ideas flow. Strive for a big number of tactical ideas (100 or more). At this point, quantity is more important than quality.

2. For starters, you might want to review your customer analysis findings to brainstorm ideas of how you can creatively execute your strategy and reach your target customers. You may also focus the brainstorming around the major steps of the funnel. And, play to your strengths. Include tactics where you perform well based on your marketing performance analysis.

3. Also, think about your proof points. What are creative ways to demonstrate your competitive advantages and communicate them (at the right stage of the buyer journey)?

4. You may want to group some of the tactics together. Select ideas that when combined, may easily form a tactical campaign. Also, this exercise is not only about the top end of the funnel. Think about your sales performance and brainstorm how to sell better, faster, and smarter.

5. Once you have a large number of ideas (100 or more), organize the ideas by category type, e.g., lead generation, sales, or by conversional funnel stages. Then, develop a set of criteria to evaluate each idea type. This is similar to the evaluation matrix method you used in Chapter 5. However, you will likely need a new set of criteria and weighting factors.

6. Now, using your new evaluation matrix tool, score each of the tactical ideas.

7. Take the highest scoring ideas and build some projections or forecasts to determine if they will generate the intended results. Ballpark implementation costs as well.

EXERCISE 7.2 PLAN
BUILDING AN INTEGRATED TACTICAL CAMPAIGN
You've honed your strategy and identified high scoring tactical support options. Now you have to pull it all together, orchestrating your marketing and sales teams to connect with customers at every touch point.

EXERCISE 7.2 CAMPAIGN PLANS
1. It is time to decide which strategy and supporting tactical actions you will deploy. So, you'll need to flesh out how these ideas will really work. And, equally important, you will need to determine when will you deploy your resources (factoring in the time it takes to build and create the tactical elements). Big objectives and clever strategies can be overwhelming. So, break down the effort into doable doses. Organizing your tactical execution by campaigns can make the initiative much more manageable. For some business models with seasonal cycles and renewal dates, organizing campaigns to match the cycle is obvious. Other business models require "artificial" cycles or events you can set as anchors. How can you organize your top scoring tactical ideas into campaigns? Are there industry events that might serve as an anchor to a possible campaign?

2. In this exercise, draft a simple tactical campaign for a particular product or service anchored around a key event. Make sure to include how you will pull, push or otherwise compel new business through the funnel. It is often helpful to have "mini" funnels for each tactical campaign. Establish target performance levels for each funnel segment, starting with the target number of closed sales. The campaign should be as detailed as necessary to achieve your objectives and might require every sales and marketing tool and trick in the book.

3. Also, give special consideration to how you coordinate the hand off of leads from marketing to sales (especially if the campaign is a change in your normal new business routine.)

4. Check your work. You should be able to trace the targeted end results of the campaign directly back to a SMART objective. The campaign should support a defined strategy that solves how you will achieve your SMART objective. If not, you need to go back to the drawing board. How close are you to your objective target? How many other campaigns are needed to accomplish it? Can you simply repeat this campaign over and over until you are there? Or, do you need to develop a different campaign?

EXERCISE 7.3 PLAN
BUILD AN ALL-STAR TEAM

So now you have some killer tactical campaigns ideas that will drive growth. But, who is going to actually launch these growth initiatives? Who is going to do the work? You'll need the right team with the right skills and strengths to bring it all to life. And, how will this impact your organizational chart?

EXERCISE 7.3 YOUR TEAM DRAFT

1. Carefully review your tactical campaigns. Identify the skills and strengths needed to successfully produce each element of the campaign.

2. Do you have these resources in-house? Or, will you need to bring in additional resources? If you must go outside of your organization, will you outsource or form strategic partnerships?

3. Draft a team roster and assign roles for each part of the campaign. I recommend adding another tab to your strategy workbook and create an org chart spreadsheet. This sheet should capture work projects, tasks and the strengths, and skill sets that you will need to successfully execute your growth initiative.

⌘

CHAPTER 7. RESOURCES

RECOMMENDED READING

The Best Little Marketing Plan, Harry, Sean, 2014.

Duct Tape Marketing, Jantshch, John, 2011.

Guerilla Marketing, Levinson, Jay, 2007.

The Marketing Plan Handbook, Chernev, Alexander, 2011.

Marketing Plans: How to Prepare Them, How to Use Them, McDonald, Malcolm, 2011.

8 YOUR GROWTH FORECAST

The only function of economic forecasting is to make astrology look respectable. -John Kenneth Gilbraith

EVERY STRATEGY and tactical plan carries its own risk and rewards. A solid forecast can help you determine if the projected rewards are sweet enough to take the risk. A forecast, if done well, is also an excellent planning tool because it answers not just what will happen, but when. Of course, peering into the future is notoriously unreliable. But, standing on top of a big pile of data and insights from your work in previous seven chapters, gives you a better vantage point. From that perspective, you will better see what lies ahead.

CHAPTER 8 OBJECTIVES
By the end of Session 8, you will have a solid draft of a growth forecast.

EXERCISE 8.1 FOCUS & PLAN
PLAYING WITH YOUR NUMBERS
Once you begin to get comfortable with your buyer journey funnels, they can be extremely powerful planning devices. They are especially helpful when exploring the financial impact of different marketing scenarios. In this exercise, you'll play the "what if" game and explore how changes in conversion rates, performance variances at each funnel segments and timing impact your objectives.

EXERCISE 8.1
1. Select one of your well-developed funnels from Exercise 6.4. Add two more columns to the funnel, one for timing and one for costs.

2. Using data from your past performance analysis and ballpark figures for the likely projected costs, estimate revenues for each stage of the funnel. Factor in estimated costs required to produce a tactical campaign.

3. Then, plug in time estimates for each funnel stage of the campaign. That is, how much time is typically required at each funnel stage?

4. Using this information, you can begin to calculate important information including cost per lead and the total cost per new customer acquisition. You will also be able to project how long the lead generation to cash cycle really is.

5. Now, have some fun with these numbers. Try adjusting conversion rates up and down and monitor the impact those changes have on your costs. Also, adjust your target objective goals and see how that impacts the funnel.

6. As a start, set your sales goal at 1 and based on your past performance conversion rates, how much activity volume is needed at each stage up the funnel to get one closed sale? How long does it typically take? How much did it cost? NOTE: In most cases, as your sales target increase, you can also generate economies of scale since most costs can be reduced with higher volume. Your objective is to build the most cost-effective revenue generation machine, one that is consistent, reliable, repeatable and predictable.

7. Do you have a set budget or past performance budget in mind? How far off budget (over or under) are you in these scenarios? Brainstorm ways you generate the same effect faster or cheaper.

8. Play around with your funnels until you find the optimal (and realistic) cost/time/benefit ratios.

EXERCISE 8.2 PLAN
BUILD YOUR FORECAST

There is simply no easy way to do this. But, the time has come to build your growth projections to determine if your strategy and supporting tactics will actually generate the growth revenue you need when you need it.

EXERCISE 8.2

1. Create a simple spreadsheet using a basic pro forma style that coincides with the time period of your SMART objectives. At the top will be your revenue with sub line items for revenue sources (as detailed as you need). Under that, detail your costs for marketing and sales line items (preferably by tactical campaign). Since this is not a true P&L report, there is no need to add in your fixed costs just yet. Now add a column to the right for your forecasted time period (e.g., weekly, monthly, quarterly, etc.).

2. Next, conduct a planning session with your trusted sales and marketing team. Task them to work together to plug in the missing information using the data from past exercises, particularly 8.1, 7.2 and 6.4. Make sure to extrapolate revenue projections based on sales generated. For instance, if you project that your campaign will generate 10 closed deals for the time period, be sure to calculate how much anticipated revenue will be generated from those sales (and when that cash will hit your books).

3. Repeat this for all of the tactical campaigns necessary to fulfill the strategy during the time period. Also, factor in deals from your sales pipeline (applying whatever scoring or weighting mechanisms adopted by your business.) For businesses that religiously manage their marketing and sales pipelines using CRM systems and marketing automation, this process is much easier. By the close of the exercise, you should have a decent first draft of a forecast.

4. Then, briefly analyze the forecast and calculate a quick risk/reward assessment. Do you exceed or fall short of your objective? Does investing in this strategy yield the returns you want? Does it get you to your objectives? How will you change it to make it more effective? Where are the holes and gaps? If it isn't working, do you need to go back to evaluate other strategic options?

5. Now, share the draft of the forecast with your buddy or trusted advisor and HolePunch it? What is your confidence level in the accuracy of the forecast? What would you change to make you feel

more confident? How far out can you project – a month, a quarter, a year? Longer? The further you can see, the better

EXERCISE 8.3 FOCUS
YOUR KPI DASHBOARD

It's a cliché, but it is true: you can't manage what you don't measure. So, how are you going to measure the key steps of your growth before you roll it up into a CAGR (combined annual growth rate)? Build a real-time dashboard that displays your progress as you go.

EXERCISE 8.3

1. Build a new spreadsheet, or add a tab spreadsheet in your master plan spreadsheet.

2. Create a simple data table for each of your Key Performance Indicators (from Chapter 4) with a field for target performance levels and actual performance levels. You may also want to create a field that captures the percentage difference or percentage of for each KPI.

3. You may want to build dashboards for the entire funnel, break it down by campaign or segment.

4. Then, connect your spreadsheet to a visual display generator, such as Klipfolio.com or Domo. These simple display templates quickly and easily build visual representation dashboards of your data in real-time. This makes it fun and easy to monitor, track and share the most important data points of your plan execution. With a few simple formulas, you can also track cost per lead, cost per customer acquisition, and variance over time.

5. For organizations that already subscribe to online CRM and marketing automation software systems, most have API's or plug-ins that allow you to pull this data directly from those systems. That minimizes your manual effort.

6. Routinely check on the dashboard and make course corrections as you go. Depending on the volume of your business, you may need to monitor this information daily, weekly or monthly. You can then use this data to compare the performance of campaigns and tactics. You will also begin to identify other trends, e.g., the seasonal impact on your performance.

⌘

CHAPTER 8. RESOURCES

Table 6. KPI DASHBOARD

	Target Results	Actual Results
Date		
Objective		
KPI 1		
KPI 2		
KPI 3		
Budget		

Table 7. FORECAST TABLE (PRO FROMA PART 1)

Strategy	Q1	Q2	Q3	Q4	Year 2	Year 3
Option 1						
Option 2						
Option 3						
Total						

RECOMMENDED READING

Forecasting: Principles & Practice, Hyndman, Rob, 2013.

Sales Forecasting: A New Approach, Wallace & Stahl, 2002.

The Signal & The Noise, Silver, Nate, 2012.

9 YOUR BUDGET

Spare no expense to save money on this one. -Samuel Goldwyn

YOUR FORECAST highlights the reward of the strategy. Now you need to get a clearer picture of what you are putting at risk. Just how much of that time, talent and treasure is needed to hit your target and achieve your objectives? An accurate budget is crucial. If you estimate too high, you may not act on a strategy because the costs didn't justify it and you scrapped a strategy that otherwise might have worked well. If you estimate too low, you may also find that a campaign or tactic is insufficiently funded to produce the intended results. Carefully crafting your budget will help you find the cost/benefit equation sweet spot.

CHAPTER 9 OBJECTIVES
By the end of Session 9, you will have a fresher outlook on the budget process and a solid draft of a budget.

EXERCISE 9.1 PLAN
A BETTER BUDGET

You are actually more than half way done with your budget. In exercise 9.1, you will build a better budget; one that precisely defines the financial investment required to successfully and efficiently execute your growth plan. When you build your budget from the ground up, it becomes a financial blueprint that reflects your objectives and values giving you greater confidence and control so that your investment will yield higher returns.

EXERCISE 9.1:

1. Get in the right frame of mind. First, don't think of the budget as a constraint. Think of your budget as an investment or spending plan. It is a lot more fun that way. Next, you may be tempted to simply grab last year's budget, dust it off and add a little bump for inflation. Then, cut and paste the expenses from last year and, Voila! Your budget is down in 15 minutes. Don't do that!

    NOTE: If you are pursuing an M&A growth strategy rather than an organic growth strategy, you still need a budget. "Shopping" for a business to buy takes a lot of time and often considerable financial resources to conduct a proper due diligence review. In addition, you'll need to figure the cost of capital and professional fees of brokers, CPA's and attorneys.

2. Get detailed costs estimates for all of the line items in your tactical plan and forecast. Make sure you include internal and external labor costs.

    For instance, let's say your tactical plan requires you to generate 1,000,000 impressions in the Awareness segment of your funnel using mass media, like online radio or digital ads (depending on your target customer profiles). Now you can explore which media outlets will deliver the best impressions at the best price. Once you have sourced the best options, you will be able to use those cost estimates your budget.

3. Once you have credible cost data, plug those figures into your accounting system. Today, even entry-level accounting programs have budget capabilities. Or, if it is easier, simply keep your budget in a spreadsheet program. Remember, make sure you detail exactly when you will incur those costs in your budget. You will probably incur the costs to develop creative materials long before the actual media spend and before you actually start to generate impressions. But, all of those

costs may be associated with a tactical campaign for a specific funnel segment. Depending on how long it takes to convert a new customer from a lead generated by a brand new tactical campaign, you may cross over into next year's budget plan. That makes it a little difficult to track real ROI.

Now that you have a more accurate and detailed budget, update your forecast from exercise 8.2 and crunch your projections again. You will begin to have a very clear picture of how much you will need to invest in order to generate your target level of return. This will help you sound strategic buying decisions going forward, because you will know how much you will spend on a per lead and per new customer acquisition. So, when you are developing new growth strategies, or exploring other lead generation opportunities, you will be able to better compare costs.

⌘

CHAPTER 9. RESOURCES

Table 8. BUDGET TABLE (PRO FORMA PART 2)

Strategy	Q1	Q2	Q3	Q4	Year 2	Year 3
Option 1						
Option 2						
Option 3						
Total						
Budget						
Option 1						
Option 2						
Option 3						
Total						
Margin						

RECOMMENDED READING

Budgeting: A Comprehensive Guide (3rd Edition), Bragg, Stephen, 2014.

Total Business Budgeting (2nd Edition), Rachlin, Robert, 1999.

10 PREPARE TO LAUNCH

Think like a man of action. Act like a man of thought. -Henri Bergson

SMART OBJECTIVES? Check. Vetted strategies? Check. Detailed action plan? Check. The last thing you want to hear is, "Houston, we have a problem." So, go through and check your work. You want to make sure that you've thought through every detail and contingency so that if a problem comes up, you'll know how and who will handle it. And, don't bite off more than you can chew at the start, especially if you have struggled to meet objectives in the best. Put a win in the score column. Then, move on to the next game.

CHAPTER 10 OBJECTIVES
By the end of Chapter 10, you will be ready to launch with a:
* 90 Day Tactical Action Plan
* Proofed and polished written plan and presentation
* Organized communication approach

EXERCISE 10.1 FOCUS
YOUR FIRST 90 DAYS
It is probably no surprise that most plans, even those built on sound strategies, get off to a rocky start. To be sure, the first 90 days can be tough. Improve your chances of success with a detailed action plan for those first 90.

EXERCISE 10.1
1. Double-check your alignment. Make sure that your action plan will truly deliver the intended results in order to achieve your SMART objectives. You should see a cascading step effect if you charted the major steps like this:

SMART Objective

     Strategy

          Tactical Campaign

               90-Day Action Plan

2. Review the details of your integrated tactical campaign(s) and identify exactly what needs to be done in painstaking detail. If you have a strong project manager on your team, this is the time for her to shine. If you use a project management system, this will be a lot easier. A shared spreadsheet in a Google Drive will work – there's no need to over invest.

3. Then, define exactly when each of those tasks needs to be done from beginning to end.

4. Next, assign a person on your team who will "own" that task. You want a single point of accountability who will guarantee that the prescribed task will be done (done well), and on time. (You may want to build in some incentive rewards for those who prove to be rock stars. For sure, they deserve public accolades if not a prize.)

5. Factor in your detailed cost estimates from Exercise 9.1.

6. Carefully look at those first 30 days. Double check other initiatives, staffing levels, vacation and holiday schedules and make sure you can accomplish everything that needs to be done for that first month.

7.   Then, do the same for the next 60 days.

8.   Make sure you build in routine check-points (weekly and monthly) and commit to giving the team any guidance and help they need. Challenges, problems, and issues will come up. Be ready to help clear the deck. Remember, this is for your #1 strategic growth objectives. So, there really is nothing more important.

EXERCISE 10.2 CREATE
BRING IT ALL TOGETHER

You are so close. The heavy thought lifting is done. Now you need to package it up. If you've stayed on track and completed all of the exercises, this is easy.

EXERCISE 10.2

1. Assemble all of the plan details, strategic models, charts and tables in the order of the outline of page 15.

2. Draft any explanation sections not completed

3. Write up a brief summary (1 page) of the entire strategic plan as an executive summary. Think of it as a highlight real for the most important sections. You can even cut and paste some of the work you've already done. No need to reinvent the wheel.

4. Proof read it. Double-check the numbers. (Get another pair of eyes on this part.) You are not looking for errors in thought at this point, you are simply making sure that all of the spelling, and grammar, formatting and other protocols are properly followed.

5. Then, design it. It does not need to look like a brochure, but, it should be easy to read and visually compelling. Strive for consistency and simplicity.

6. Be prepared to run through at least 2 drafts before you've got it perfect.

7. Then, if needed, create a companion presentation to the plan. This is not intended to be a verbatim recreation of the plan in PowerPoint or Keynote. Rather, it is highlight reel of the most important parts. Always remember: keep your audience in mind and make sure they get what they need out of it. They are probably thinking: "So what? What's in it for me?" Tell your story with those questions in mind and you'll be just fine.

Now, what's next? Take a moment to admire your plan. Then, go do it!

Be bold. Grow.

⌘

CHAPTER 10. RESOURCES

Table 9. YOUR 30-60-90 DAY ACTION PLANNER

Smart objective	Insert your well-defined, **strategic** SMART objective here.		
Strategy	Insert a brief summary of your strategy here. Or insert a code name for that strategy.		
Tactical objective	Insert well-defined and specific SMART **tactical** objectives here.		
Tactical plan	**30 Day**	**60 Day**	**90 Day**
	(date)	(date)	(date)
Single point of accountability (SPA)	*Identify the project leader*		
Action steps	*Define required action steps*		
KPI	*Insert current progress relative to KPI targets*		
Status update	*Insert project results to date (red, yellow or green light)*		
Corrective action required	*Insert actions to correct any problems*		
Budget	*Insert current spending levels relative to the plan budget*		

RECOMMENDED READING

The New One Page Project Manager, Campbell, 2012.

Scrappy Project Management, Wiefling, Kimberly, 2007.

Strategic Project Management Made Simple, Schmidt, Terry, 2009.

ABOUT THE AUTHOR

TIM KINNEY is the founder and president of Kinney Strategy. He is a writer, speaker and consultant specializing in strategic growth planning. With over 25 years of experience, Tim has earned his place as a trusted advisor to business leaders facing complex challenges. His approach has helped clients generate hundreds of millions in new growth.

He lives in St. Augustine, Florida with his wife, Andrea and son, Jake.

www.ingramcontent.com/pod-product-compliance
Lightning Source LLC
Chambersburg PA
CBHW060400190526
45169CB00002B/685